Setup a Point Website Today:

Install WordPress, Create Massive Content, Secure and Backup Your Blog WITHOUT Being a Computer Geek

By Robert Plank
www.BackupCreator.com

© 2012 by Robert Plank, (408) 277-0904
Learn more at: www.RobertPlank.com

I want to help you get your website online and set up in a way that, any time you want to change the look and feel, add a new section, or add new content, you can do so very quickly and easily.

We're going to be using a tool called WordPress. It's a free tool, and when you set it up in the correct way, you can put this on a website that you personally own.

You have full control over the way it looks, what content's in there, and if you are a really advanced user, you can even hire editors and authors to create your content for you.

You can have visitors stop by your site and leave constructive comments and feedback. You can link to other sites and basically create anything you want on the Internet, without knowing coding, without knowing any kind of fancy tools. Install the site, including domains.

There are a few things you need to know about the Internet before you even think about creating a website. The first thing you need to know is what a domain name is. This is a .com name. For example, If you go to a site like Google.com, they, at some point, had registered a web address or a .com or a domain name.

This is what you need to do, when you are creating your very own site on the Internet. When you create your domain name, get a website online and have your WordPress blog installed, you can get this all done in a few minutes and the good news is you will not have to hire an outsourced worker or a webmaster to make the changes in your site for you.

Install the Site

It's all a point and click site. It's very important that you get your website set up and you install WordPress, that way it's done in a few minutes, and you can easily make changes. Here's what you need to do.

You need to register a domain name. This is the .com name where people will find you on the Internet. You need to sign up for a web host, or a place to store your files on the Internet, and you need to install the WordPress platform.

A domain name, a .com name will run you about ten dollars per year. A webhost will run you about five to ten dollars per month, and WordPress is 100% free.

You register your domain name first, then you get an account at a webhost, and tell them what your domain name is. Usually, they'll give you instructions on how to point your domain name to their webhost, and then you will be ready to install WordPress, so that you can create your website content and have a website ready to go.

Here's how you do it. First, open up your web browser and go to NameCheap.com, and find out if the domain name that you want is available. The bad news is, many domain names are still taken, but the good news is, if you find a .com name that's free, people will easily be able to remember it, because most people know to go to the .com.

Try searching your first and last name. Now, if that's taken, maybe you want to make it your first and last name blog.com. I find that, many times, I have to try 20, 30, or 50 different combinations, until I find something that's available.

Then I grab that domain name from NameCheap, and then go to HostGator.com. That will host my website for me. When you go to

HostGator, you click on "View Webhosting Plans" and sign up with their baby plan. If you pay it month to month, it's only $8 per month.

Once you order a webhost from them, you tell them you currently have a domain name, type in your domain name right there, and continue on to create a username, fill in your billing details, and it's just that easy. They will bill you once a month to keep your files online.

It's very important that you register your .com name separately from your webhost, so that way, you have full control over both. Some webhosts will try to register your domain name for you, and the problem with that is you can't leave or change webhosts in the future.

If you stop paying for your webhost, you lose your domain name as well. This way, you will have all the freedom you want to move to a different webhost in the future.

Now what you have done is registered an address on the Internet. This is your domain name or your .com name. You are now paying monthly for a webhost, such as HostGator, and the next thing you want to do is put something onto our website.

Luckily, setting up WordPress is very easy. You are setting up a blog, which displays different posts or journal entries and pages or navigation on the Internet. By setting up WordPress, you will be able to log into what's called a backend area, and moderate different comments, change or add or delete different posts, and change the design of your site, just by clicking around.

You might have heard of WordPress. You might have heard of blogger site such as Blogger, but you want to have the self-hosted WordPress version. If you go to WordPress.com, you've gone to the wrong place.

WordPress.com tries to host a blog for you, but you want to host your blog on your own website. That way, you can do whatever you want with it. You can install whatever plugins, whatever themes, add whatever you want to.

Instead of WordPress.com, you should go to WordPress.org. Now, how do you set up WordPress? Well, the easy way is to go to whatever your website is called and then go to /cpanel. For example, MembershipNewbie.com/cpanel.

Now, when you sign up to HostGator, you create a username and password to log into, this cpanel, this Control Panel. Once you log in, you can scroll down and find a smiley face that says, "Fantastico Deluxe."

Click on that, and then click on WordPress. By filling in a simple form, you can create your blog at the top level of your website. Fill in a username and password, and now you have a blog completely set up.

Once you have your WordPress website set up, on your webhost, which you use along with your domain name, now you will be able to log into one central place and edit and change and update your website.

Go to NameCheap to register your address or your .com name on the Internet. Then go to HostGator, so that that .com name has some place to go, and in that process, they might give you what's called DNS information, but just follow their simple instructions. Then you will be able to create your very own WordPress website.

Control Panel Basics

Congratulations! You've set up your WordPress website, and now you need to figure out how to use it. If you set this up properly, your WordPress site is now at "yourwebsite.com."

You can see that there is just one piece of content on there and nothing to really do, but you want to log into the site, and you can do that by going to "yourwebsite.com/wp-admin."

We're going to be looking around the WordPress backend, and figuring out how to add and change content on our site. You go to yourwebsite.com/wp-admin, and you are now logged into your WordPress website.

There are many things to click on, but on the left sidebar, there are only a handful of things you need to worry about. For example, there's a "Settings" area, where you can change the title of your site.

There's a "Posts" area, where you can add journal entries or content, and a Comments area, where you can view the feedback or comments that other people have given you.

This is a heads up display of your site, so at any given moment, you can see what content's on there and what people have said. When you filled in your WordPress site, when you set it up, hopefully you set it up at the top level or root of your domain name, such as "MembershipNewbie.com," where I've set up my blog.

Go to your website /wp-admin, and now you're in what's called your WordPress dashboard. Keep in mind that the username and password you use to log into your WordPress dashboard is different than the username and password for your webhosting control panel.

Now, you logged into your site /wp-admin, and we're going to change a few posts and a few comments. I like to have my forward facing website, myname.com, in one browser tab, and my WordPress dashboard in another tab.

That way, I can make changes on one and view them on another. Now, by default, WordPress adds a post that says, "Hello, World!" and we can go ahead and delete that.

You click on the "Posts" link, find the "Hello, World!" post, click on the Trash button, and now you have no posts left in your blog. Refresh the site, and now nothing has been found on the site.

Now, if you want to add a new journal entry to your site, it's very easy. On the left sidebar, go to Posts > Add New, and then we can say, "My Latest Update," for the title, and "Here is my latest update," for the content of the message.

If we do nothing else at that point, you click "Publish," refresh the site, and now your latest update is right there, online. I know many people whose blogs solely consist of quotes and videos that they've found along the Internet, but they're all organized in one place.

Unlike social networks, like Facebook, these are easy to find later, they get indexed by search engines, and if you want to link to other websites, you can. This includes affiliate links, products and ads and other ways that you can get paid later, from your site.

By setting up your WordPress site in the proper way, you can now update it from anywhere. You can do several different things, such as moderating comments. If I go back to my site and click on any post, by default, WordPress will allow people to leave comments underneath any piece of content you have.

If you say, "Wow, nice site" in a comment, it will be posted and, by default, this will be held for moderation. This means that, if you're worried about people spamming your site or leaving rude comments, they are dependent on you to say that comment is okay.

In your WordPress dashboard, there is a sidebar link that says Comments. Click on that, and it will list all the most recent comments on your site. You can see the name of the person, their website address if they left one, where they are in the world, and you can choose to approve it, trash it, or mark it as spam, meaning that that person will not be able to post on your blog again.

It's pretty easy, pretty point and click, as long as you're careful about what you click around on, but if you keep in mind that the very basics of your WordPress control panel are adding and editing posts and moderating comments, life will be a lot easier for you.

One thing I also want to bring to your attention is the reason we use the WordPress platform, instead of many other platforms, is because of these things called "plugins."

With WordPress, you can install many, many different plugins to do anything you'd ever want. For example, if you want to add a popup to your WordPress blog, there's a plugin for that.

If you want to add a discussion board or a forum to your site, there's a plugin for that. Just go to Plugins, Add New, and you can search if you want to find some specific functionality, or just browse at the most popular plugins for things like content forums, image galleries, traffic statistics, caching, social media, link checking, and much more.

I want to be very clear that there are two different dashboards here. You have your website control panel, where you can change files, change your password on the entire account and install WordPress, and once you have installed WordPress, you now have your WordPress dashboard, which is where you manage content.

There are two different areas of your site to log in: at yoursite.com/cpanel, which controls your entire webhosting account, and then yoursite.com/wp-admin, which is where you manage your content, manage your blog, which is your online journal.

I hope that now you understand the basics of your WordPress control panel, and now you can update from anywhere, from any browser, without having to install any software, and now you can begin building out a real quality site.

Content Links and Images

There is really no point in setting up a website unless you have something to say, unless your website actually says something. What is great about the Internet is that everyone is on a level playing field, and if you have something to say, that thing is now publicly accessible from anywhere on the Internet.

It's very easy. Log into your WordPress dashboard, by going to yoursite.com/wp-admin, go to Posts > Add New, and start talking about whatever subject you want to talk about today.

I know many people will simply write an article right in WordPress. Now, at any point, if you need to pick up on that post later, you click the Save Draft button and your post is not yet live on your site.

Now, by having a site that you can update anytime, anywhere you want, you can provide value to other people on the Internet. There are many sites like TechCrunch or The Huffington Post, which are blogs that just report about happenings around the world and around the Internet.

They don't always have to think of their own material. They just report on different things that are happening all around the world. They take similar steps to you.

They go to Posts > Add New, they decide on what title they want and what post content they want, and it doesn't need to be any more complicated than that. If you need a simple way to make a blog post, go to a site like YouTube.com and grab a random video that you can now put onto your website.

If I was going to search for a video on how to tie a tie, I could just go to YouTube, search that in the box and click on the video that I want. If this is something that I want to put onto my own site, I can just click on the address in the address bar of my browser, right click and copy, then go to my post and title it, "How to Tie a Tie."

Then, in the body of the post, right click and paste. As soon as I publish this blog post, the video will be directly in the post. I click View Post, and now my top piece of content is a video showing how to tie a tie.

This is the process of adding a new post. If you want to add extra navigation to your site, that's also very easy. Go to your dashboard and go to Pages, Add New.

Now, you do not want to add too many pages of your website. If you have something that is very important that you want everyone to always be able to see, you can add an About page or a Contact page.

Go to Pages > Add New and type in About Me, and then type in your bio "Here is my bio information". Click on Publish, and when you go back to your site, in the top navigation, there is an About Me page that anyone can get back to.

Posts are regular updates, journal entries that you make on a regular basis, but a page is top-level navigation that might be something like an About Me page. The only tricky part is knowing where to go.

To add a new post, go to Posts > Add New, type in your title, your content, and then publish it. I want to let you in on an advanced secret with WordPress. You can schedule content out in the future, without very much work at all.

I will give you an example. Let's say I wanted to make another post about how to tie a bow tie, and I grab the link that I want. I can put that in a post and call it, "How to Tie a Bow Tie" and instead of publishing this immediately, I can change the date that it will be published into the future.

WordPress will automatically drip it out. What this means is that no one will be able to see the post until the date I want. On that date, they magically will be able to see it.

Now that you know how to easily add content to your blog, any time you have something to say, everyone will be able to see it. You will be able to post this on social media sites, Facebook it, re-tweet it, post it to Google Plus. If anyone wants to link to it, they can get right back to your site.

What about making your website search engine friendly? If someone is searching for a subject , for example, how to tie a bow tie, how do you make sure that your blog pages and posts appear at the top of these Google search results? That's where Search Engine Optimization comes in.

Search Engine Optimization

I'm not sure if you've heard the term "search engine optimization" before, but you want to make sure that search engines love your WordPress site. This means you have to follow a few simple rules of the Internet, and you will be rewarded with link backs, with traffic, and hopefully many people coming to your site.

Search engine optimization is important because you need to set up your site in a certain site and name your posts in a certain way so that other people can find you and recommend you.

There's a very simple change you can make to your WordPress site, and that's by giving your site friendly links or permalinks. By default, when you set up a WordPress blog, they will add numeric addresses on your posts.

This means that if I make a new post, it might call the address P=8, P=2, P=10, but you're going to get a boost in your search engine rankings if the exact address for your post contains some of the words you talk about.

For example, if I have a blog post called "How to Tie a Tie," I want that exact post to be located at MembershipNewbie.com/how-to-tie-a-tie. Search engines love it when your posts are named in their link exactly as they are in the actual post.

This is very easy to set up. Go to Settings > Permalinks, and choose Post Name. You can see that, depending on how you name your content, what the title of your post is, they will change what your web address is.

By changing your permalink to run in post name, now your website addresses will be named the same as the content. Click Save Changes, and we view our blog again.

We can see that our addresses for each individual post are named very similarly to the title of our actual post. Our About Me page is now at oursite.com/about-me. This will give you a huge boost in the rankings in addition to the boosts you already have from using a WordPress site in the first place.

Let me tell you about how to name your posts in addition to this. Do a search for Google External Keyword Tool. If you have an idea for a new blog post, you can type in a few possible titles or phrases and Google will tell you what are the more competitive phrases and what the more high traffic phrases are.

If I type in quotes, "How to Tie a Tie", type in quotes, "How to Tie a Bow Tie," type in quotes, "Tying a Tie," and I perform a quick search, they will give me an idea of possibly titling the post "How to Tie a Bow Tie Video."

The problem is that not very many people are searching for that. What people are searching for are things like: "How to Tie a Tie," "How to Knit," "How to Tie a Necktie," "Tying a Tie," "How to Tie a Bow Tie," "How to Tie Bow Ties," "Tie Neckties," "How to Tie Scarves."

You could possibly create different posts or different videos on each of these different subjects. A video about how to tie a necktie or on different kinds of knots, and before you make your exact post, do a quick check and see what suggestions they give you.

You can make a blog post about tying skinny ties, clip-on neckties, different knots for neckties, a Windsor tie, and if you had just gone ahead and called your blog post "How to Tie a Tie," you only would have had one piece of content out there.

Now that you've done a little bit of searching, you can see which key words are very competitive. "Where to Buy Bow Ties" might be too competitive a keyword for not very many monthly searches, but then you see that there are key phrase suggestions for "neckties" or "men's ties," and now you can see what is popular and what is in demand.

Just titling your blog posts correctly will give you a huge boosts. Having those permalinks set correctly, by going to Settings, Permalinks, and changing your permalink type to Post Name will help.

Now, here is something else many people don't know, even experienced WordPress users, is that you can control what your posts are addressed as. You can control your linking structure.

Go to Posts > Edit a Post, and underneath your post title, there's an area that says Permalink. Now, they will show you what is the exact web address or URL of this post. By clicking Edit, you can change the exact web address of your individual post.

I would highly recommend you not changing a post if it's been live for more than a day. If you decide that a particular web address on your blog is too long or you want to change it to something, like "How to Tie a Necktie," you can change the address of this exact post by editing the post, editing the permalink of the post, and then clicking on Update to save your changes.

That will really help you to get your website optimized, targeting the right keywords and having good content. One other thing I want to show you is how to group your posts together into categories.

When you create a new post, you can scroll down on the right side. There is a list of categories this post belongs to. You might want to add a category for personal different posts, a category for tips, a category for resources, and a category for videos. When you make a new blog post, you can pick and choose which areas of your site this applies to.

That means if you were, for example, making a blog about personal hygiene, you can have a group of posts on how to clean clothes, how to tie a tie, and how to take care of your skin. People could easily navigate to any part of the site that they want.

They go to your site and they can click on the category that they want to list all of the particular posts in that category. I hope that once you understand a lot of the different lingo, such as choosing your keywords, setting up your permalinks, and having categories set up, then you can get a lot more traffic just by doing the things that most people don't like to do.

Do a quick double check to make sure that you've chosen a good keyword, have a good linking structure, and make sure that your posts are relevant and categorized in an easy way.

Now that you have set up your site and you're good at managing your content, let's change some of the functionality of your site by installing a few WordPress plugins.

Top WordPress Plugins

One of the best features, if not the best feature, of WordPress is that in just a few seconds you can install almost any additional functionality to your website. In the past, you used to have to find a programmer and pay them hundreds, if not thousands of dollars to set up, debug, and create a discussion board software or to give people the ability to comment or to add popups.

Now, with WordPress, you can just add any functionality of your site that you want. Before we get to plugins themselves, let's try customizing your WordPress sidebar. It is very easy. Go to your WordPress dashboard. Remember, it is at yoursite.com/wp-admin.

Go to Appearance in the sidebar and Widgets. This might look like a crazy difficult screen at first, but with WordPress, you can change the different sections of your sidebar. What does this mean?

It means that if you want to link to different sites in your sidebar, you just drag a box over it. If you want to list the most recent posts or comments, show a calendar of your different posts, or add a search box, you just use this widget area and customize and drag and drop and rearrange the different parts of your WordPress site.

Here is how easy it is. Once you are in the Appearance Widgets area, you will see that in the middle of the screen there are different available widgets. On the right side is your main sidebar.

If I want to add a search box to my site, I find the search box, click and drag into that main sidebar. Now when I view my site, I can see that I have a search box on the sidebar.

If I want to list my most recent posts, I find the Recent Posts widget, click, drag to the sidebar, release, and now I have a list of the recent posts on my blog. I can list my most recent categories and I can list the most recent comments. Now, my site is completely customized.

Let's say I wanted to link to other websites on the Internet. I'd go to the Links widget, click and drag to the sidebar. When I want to link to other sites, I go to the Links area on the sidebar and click Add New. Then, just type in the name of the link I want, plus the web address.

If I wanted to link to Robert Plank's blog, I would type that in and enter the web address there. If I wanted to link to Lance Tomashiro's blog, I would type in that name and then enter the web address of Lance Tomashiro there.

If I wanted to link to a WordPress plugin we have, called Backup Creator, I would type in the name of that link and the web address there. Because I have that Links widget in the sidebar, those links automatically show up on my WordPress sidebar.

If I ever want to go back and change those links, I just click on the Links link on the sidebar and I can choose which ones I want to remove or change and update or anything in between.

That's how we change our sidebar. But what about adding in, for example, a contact form on our site? This is actually very easy. You go to Plugins > Add New, and you can search for anything you want.

For example, if I wanted to add in a plugin, add a Facebook "Like" button to my posts, type in the word "Facebook," click Search Plugins, and it lists over a thousand plugins for Facebook. Some of them do more functionality than others, but this is how to find thousands and thousands of free plugins.

Let's do something useful, like adding a contact form. Go to Plugins > Add New. In the search box, type "Contact Form," click Search Plugins and this will list many, many different contact forum plugins that will install on top of your site in just one click.

Click Install Now, and in just a few seconds this has now installed a contact form plugin. Click Activate Plugin, and now we have to find the settings for this contact form. Just look around the sidebar.

It might be under the Settings menu, the Tools menu, or it might have a menu of its own. Then they will have instructions, usually right in the plugin. This particular plugin for a contact form says to put a short code onto our posts that's [contact_form].

Click and hold down, select this code they want us to use, right click and copy, go to Pages > Add New, call the page Contact Form, paste in what's called that short code, and make sure that we change the permalink to something that we can use.

I'm going to change this permalink to /contact, so if someone goes to MembershipNewbie.com/contact, they can send me an email without me exposing my email address.

Click Publish, and when I view that page, we can see that someone can fill in their name, email address, subject and their message, and send me anything that they want.

If they go to the front page of my site, because this is a page, it appears as part of the navigation. Now, let's say I wanted someone to be able to send me a message but not be able to comment.

It's very easy. Click Edit Page, and we want to not allow people to comment. Click on Screen Options at the top, click on Discussion, and when we update the page, we can now uncheck Allow Comments. By checking that and viewing the page again and saving it, we can now see that we have a WordPress page that does not allow comments.

You can see that you have 100 percent control over your site with simple point and click functionality. You add pages, you add posts, and you can even turn off comments for your entire blog or just individual pieces of content, and your plugins work seamlessly with your look and feel and with your posts as well.

Many of these plugins use these things called copy and paste short codes so that you can embed a contact form anywhere on your site. Let's do something else fun with plugins and add an anti-spam plugin.

You go to the Plugins area, and by default, WordPress should have an anti-spam plugin called Akismet. If this, for some reason, is not on your site, go to Plugins > Add New, and search Akismet.

It looks like the settings for this are under Plugins > Akismet Configuration. They will require you to activate your Akismet plugin. They will want you to set up an account with their website, and you might have to log in and copy a piece of code from their site, but adding that will allow your comments to be checked for spam.

If your blog catches someone posting junk comments all around the Internet and then they come to your site, they will automatically be held for moderation in your spam area. You can click on Comments, click over to the Spam tab and find out if something has been incorrectly marked as spam, or delete it permanently.

I hope you understood how easy it was to add a functionality and to add plugins to your WordPress site. You go to Plugins > Add New, and then search for whatever you want.

We have been talking about search engine optimization, or SEO. If you search for plugins there, you might find different SEO plugins. My favorite is called All In One SEO.

You find the plugin you want, All In One SEO Pack, click Install Now and in just a few seconds, now that plugin has been installed, you can have full control over whatever this plugin does. In this case, it makes your site appear search engine friendly.

Now, on the off chance that you bought a paid plugin, you can go to Plugins > Add New, click the Upload tab, and then upload a ZIP file that they give you and install anything onto your WordPress blog.

When you do this, you now can add anything onto your site. But, be very careful. The more things your site does, the more vulnerable it is to attack. That's why the next thing you want to do is figure out how to secure your blog and keep it 100 percent safe from hackers.

WordPress Security

Every now and then, you might hear about some high profile website like the FBI, CIA or the White House, that has been hacked by hackers. The fact is that high profile sites are hacked into every day and millions and millions of dollars are lost because of simple security holes that could have been filled.

For example, the Reuter's news service was hacked, just because they were using an out of date version of WordPress. The harsh reality is that people find new ways of getting into websites all the time. We just have to stay updated, in order to keep our websites safe.

Staying updated is very easy. Log into your WordPress dashboard at yoursite.com/wp-admin. Go to Dashboard and then Updates. If your version is out of date, they will give you a button to upgrade. Even if your version is up to date and you are worried that you might have been compromised, you can click on the Reinstall Now button.

It will download and reinstall the version of WordPress to make sure that you have a nice and clean version. Once again, Dashboard > Updates, and you can make sure that your theme or your design, your plugins, and your WordPress version is up to date.

In addition to keeping everything up to date, there are a few things you can do right now that will keep your website safe. The first thing is be very careful where you're logging into your site.

I keep telling you that if you go to yoursite.com/wp-admin, you can do anything you want to your site. The problem is, that if you log into your site from a public place, like a library or an Internet cafe, and leave yourself logged in, other people can then make any of those changes to your site, including adding their own content or taking your entire site down.

In addition, if you log into your WordPress site from a public location, like a coffee shop, over unsecured, wireless Internet, they can also grab your password that way. It's a very good idea to not log into your WordPress site remotely, and it's a good idea to have a smart password for your WordPress site.

What do I mean by a smart password? I mean, if your username to your WordPress site is "admin", and your password is also "admin", or your username is "test" and your password is "test", these are some of the first passwords that hackers guess.

You should have a very, very long password that only you know, that only you remember. I have friends who sometimes remember an entire phrase, and their password is just the first letter out of each sentence in their phrase.

What I mean by that is, for example, if you have a phrase such as "It takes one to know one," then your password is "itotko". I know some people who sometimes will have a word and move their finger and type in the letter just to the left or just to the right of that key.

There's lots of crazy things that you can do, but just make sure that your password is not your name, your birthdate, your pet's name, because those are the most common things.

Choose some random object that you know you will always remember and a four or five digit number to put at the end of that. That is a good way to have a secure password that no one will possibly guess.

Now that you know how to log into your WordPress dashboard in public, and you have a smart password, be very, very careful of installing strange themes or installing too many WordPress plugins. These might have what are called "back doors" that will allow anyone, such as a hacker, into your site.

What's great about WordPress is that, by default, the website looks very nice. You can change the look, feel, design, and theme of the site very quickly. In your WordPress dashboard, go to Appearance > Themes.

It will list the current theme, and if you scroll down, it will list other themes that are installed. You can click Activate, switch to your site, and even though all of your content remains where it is, your links, pages, navigation, widgets, and your comments, have all remained the same. However, the way the site looks has changed.

You've just changed themes. If you want to have more themes to choose from, click on the Install Themes tab and you can choose the featured themes, click around, and find the colors you want then, want, and then click Install Now.

Give it a second to download, click Activate, and we'll go back to our site. Now we can see that, once again, the content is all still there, but the design has changed. You can change your blog theme as much as you want, until you find the one that you like.

I know many people who change their blog theme every month, and it doesn't hurt your rankings at all. It just changes the way your site looks to people who come to your site.

It's great that you can choose any theme, and many of these themes have built-in tools to make your site even more powerful. But, you need to be very careful about new or untested plugins and themes.

Here is what I mean. If someone gives you a random theme or plugin to install on your website, make sure that it's from a trusted source, a trusted friend, or that many other people have used it.

When you go to install a new theme, and you search in the WordPress area, you can click on the details and see how high it's rated and how many people have rated this particular theme.

I would prefer that you only get themes that have at least four stars and at least have a handful of people who have downloaded and used this theme. The same goes for plugins.

Go to Plugins > Add New and look at the different WordPress plugins available. If a plugin has thousands and thousands of ratings, chances are, it has been thoroughly tested and many people use it. But, if you happen to find a plugin that is out of date or that no one uses, then you might be in big trouble.

The problem is that anyone can submit a plugin for use in WordPress. A plugin has the capability to take over your entire WordPress blog. That means that if you install an untested theme or plugin and you're not careful, someone can get access to your entire site, change your site, lock you out of your own site, or shut down your site.

What I mean is that if a plugin has a low rating or only a few ratings, don't install it. Only install the most popular plugins and plugins that have been used and updated recently.

I don't want you to spend every waking moment worrying about whether your website is secure or not. Sometimes people still get through. But by doing these few things, by having a long password, by being sure not to log in from a public area, and looking at the reviews of themes and plugins and ratings before you install them, will really go a long way to keeping your website online.

You have put a lot of effort into keeping your website up to date, making it your home on the Internet, making it a site that you're proud of, you don't want it to all be gone instantly tomorrow.

Do those few things to secure your website, and it's a good idea to be safe instead of sorry and be paranoid about keeping your website safe. That means that, in addition to securing your WordPress blog, you should back it up as well.

How to Backup WordPress

The truth is, you really can't trust computers. Computers fail all the time. Hard drives crash, earthquakes and fires happen. You can't depend on your computer or even your web host to keep your website from going down at some point.

That means that you have to backup your website. The good news is that there are many backup plugins that you can install. Most of them have an automatic feature.

You install the plugin, you tell it how often you want it to backup, and in many cases, where you want to send the back up offsite. Then you don't have to worry any more about keeping your website safe and having that ability to put your website back online, in case you ever lose it.

Hopefully you won't lose it, but chances are you've been in a situation where you accidentally deleted an old file, or you want to roll back to an earlier version of your website, before you broke it. That's where backups really come in handy.

I just want to say that everything you do needs to have at least one copy. Install a backup program, such as Carbonite, on your home computer. That way, you don't lose any files on your computer.

When you log into your website control panel, yoursite.com/cpanel, go to the backups area and run a backup and save it right now, so you don't lose your site. Install a backup plugin in WordPress.

That way, every day or every week you can have an offsite copy of your site, complete with all your themes, plugins, settings and content, and restore it any time that you want.

Here's a bonus feature of many backup plugins. You can also clone, duplicate, or copy a site. This means if I set up a site on a domain like

MembershipNewbie.com and I want to copy this over to a site like RobertPlank.com, all I have to do is install a backup plugin on Membership Newbie.

Backup my site, copy the backup file over to RobertPlank.com, click the Restore button, and now I've copied my site, complete with posts, pages, themes, plugins, files—everything.

Think about what this means for you. It means that if you set up a site, get it tweaked and changed exactly the way that you want it, you can set up a second site just like it without having to go back and retrace your steps.

If you can set up a site that looks great, that's filled with content, that even maybe takes orders, backup that site, get someone to pay you to set up a similar site, and all you have to do is set up WordPress on that new location and restore your backup.

Let me tell you how to do all this. You install my backup plugin, that's called BackupCreator.com, that you can locate at BackupCreator.com. This is a WordPress Plugin that you can easily install, because I give you a ZIP file.

Installing this plugin is very easy. You go to yoursite.com/wp-admin, go to Plugins > Add New > Upload, and you can upload the plugin that I give you. Once you have this plugin online and uploaded, you can then just start your first backup.

It only takes a few seconds, and once you backup your site, you can then save it to your hard drive and upload it to FTP or Amazon S3, if you know how to use that.

It's very simple, it's one click, then you don't have to think about it anymore. Click Backup This Site, and Backup Creator will restore everything in one central ZIP file.

Your site might be small or big, and that will change the size of the file, but you can download the backup and then install it somewhere else, whenever you want.

It might seem silly to spend a few minutes every week setting up a site, or even if you set up your site, to automatically backup, to send you an email of the backup, to put it on another website, to send it to Amazon.

It might seem silly to set it up, but wouldn't you rather have a backup of your website and not need it every day, than to one day need a backup of your site and not have it?

Get it right now, install a WordPress blog at one of your websites. Now, remember, you get a domain name at NameCheap.com. Grab a domain name, a .com name, that hopefully has your name in it, possibly your brand, that isn't taken and that is also not a registered trademark with the USPTO.gov.

Register that domain name at NameCheap. Get a webhosting account at HostGator. Go into the cpanel area, use Fantastico to install a WordPress blog at the very top level of your site, and start playing around with a point and click website.

Figure out how to log in, how to add links, how to add videos, and how to add content. Put them in categories, schedule content, add pages, change your linking structure for search engine optimization, and add plugins for things like SEO, contact forms, spam protection.

Be very careful about securing your blog, because you've created a site you're proud of, and you want to protect it. Just in case anything goes wrong, if your web host fails, you accidentally delete something, or you get hacked, keep a backup of your brand new point and click WordPress website by going to BackupCreator.com.

Now, you have your own point and click website set up and you can add as much content as you want. You can schedule as much content into the future every day or every week. You can even add additional users to your website. Think about this. You can add a contributor user to your website.

You can give someone new a login and password to your site, and they can submit new content for you to approve and make the site almost update itself. You can browse through any plugin in the plugins directory of WordPress.

Add any functionality you want into your WordPress site, whether that's a contact form, a caching plugin, an e-commerce plugin, where you can take orders, different anti-spam plugins, security plugins, forums, and plugins to help with site navigation.

The choice is yours, where you take your site from here on out, but the most important thing is that you actually take action and set up your point and click website today.

Get a domain name, get a web host, go on your control panel, set up WordPress, start adding in content, and now you've created a website that costs almost nothing to set up, that costs almost nothing to maintain, that you can keep going without having to pay someone to figure out all the technical details.

It's all very common sense—point and click. I'm Robert Plank. Go ahead, do it right now, and set up your point and click website today.

About the Author

Robert Plank runs a million dollar business on the Internet creating information products, software tools, and webinar training.

He can show you how to not only save time in your business and everyday life, but do more in less time. Master WordPress. Build your list. Create passive income from information products. Generate residual income using membership sites. Scale and talk to use audiences using webinars. And more!

Robert's Online Presence:

- Blog: www.robertplank.com
- Podcast: www.robertplankshow.com/itunes
- Fan Page: www.robertplankshow.com

Robert Plank's other titles on Amazon.com:

- 100 Time Savers: Start Less, Finish More, and Cut 10 Minutes a Day from Your Schedule to Gain 60 Hours of Free Time Per Year
- Article Crash Course: Get Published, Get Instant Authority and Become an Expert in Any Subject
- Double Agent Marketing: Live the Double Life, Control Your Destiny and Become a Self-Employed Entrepreneur By Starting Your Own Home-Based Internet Information Business
- Four Daily Tasks: Overcome All Internal Roadblocks Using a Few Simple Rules, Solve Any Personal Problems and Keep Moving in a "Forward" Direction in 10 Easy Steps
- Internet Marketing on Crack: Master Your Time Management, Marketing, Sales, Traffic, Products, Customer Relationships & More From Just a Few Simple Breakthroughs
- List, Traffic & Offers: The Internet Marketing Profit Shortcut

- Membership Cube: How to Create a Passive Income in Just a Few Simple Clicks
- Secret Conversations with Internet Millionaires: How to Make Money Online with an Internet Marketing Business
- Sell on Amazon FBA: Easy Steps to Create an Online Passive Income Amazon Business with Retail Arbitrage & Private Label Sourcing
- Setup a Point & Click Website Today: Install WordPress, Create Massive Content, Secure and Backup Your Blog WITHOUT Being a Computer Geek

Robert's courses:

- Membership Cube: setup a recurring membership site
- Income Machine: establish your online system including your blog, traffic, opt-in page, autoresponder sequence and more
- Dropship CEO: sell physical products on Amazon.com
- Make a Product: self-publish a book (physical and digital) on Amazon.com
- Profit Dashboard: earn money from Fiverr
- Podcast Crusher: create your own podcast

Discover more about him at RobertPlank.com/about and contact him at RobertPlank.com/ask if you have a personal question, want to appear on his podcast, want him on your podcast, or if you wish to enquire about availability for speaking engagements.

www.ingramcontent.com/pod-product-compliance
Lightning Source LLC
LaVergne TN
LVHW052126070326
832902LV00038B/3965

It's possible to setup an entire website in just a few minutes, using free tools, without hiring a web designer or a programmer -- and now you have a beautiful looking site that does everything you want.

How is this possible? Setup your web hosting today, install WordPress and use the plugins and tools shown this book to get the best possible website setup, and do it fast.

Robert Plank has setup thousands of websites and coded several WordPress plugins and themes. He knows everything there is to know about setting up a profitable and good-looking website fast, so you'll be able to do it too.

Inside "Setup a Point & Click Website Today" you'll discover...

* How to get your website setup today in the next few minutes
* How to create massive content that bring you search engine visitors
* How to secure your website from hackers
* How to automatically backup your site so you never lose anything on it

"Setup a Point & Click Website Today" will tell you exactly what you need to know to install WordPress, get the right plugins setup, fill it with content, get search engine traffic, secure it, and back it up!

ISBN 9781481808460

90000

9 781481 808460